MW01005847

ALIVE

ALIVE

A COLD-CASE APPROACH
TO THE RESURRECTION

J. WARNER
WALLACE

David C Cook®

transforming lives together

ALIVE
Published by David C Cook
4050 Lee Vance Drive
Colorado Springs, CO 80918 U.S.A.

Integrity Music Limited, a Division of David C Cook
Brighton, East Sussex BN1 2RE, England

The graphic circle C logo is a registered trademark of David C Cook.

All rights reserved. Except for brief excerpts for review purposes,
no part of this book may be reproduced or used in any form
without written permission from the publisher.

The website addresses recommended throughout this book are offered as a
resource to you. These websites are not intended in any way to be or imply an
endorsement on the part of David C Cook, nor do we vouch for their content.

Unless otherwise noted, all Scripture quotations are taken from the
New American Standard Bible®, Copyright © 1960, 1995 by The
Lockman Foundation. Used by permission. (www.Lockman.org.)

ISBN 978-0-7814-1119-6
eISBN 978-0-7814-1128-8

© 2014 J. Warner Wallace
Published in association with the literary agency of Mark Sweeney and
Associates, 28540 Altessa Way, Apt. 201, Bonita Springs, FL 34135.
Portions of *Alive* have been taken from *Cold-Case Christianity*, published by
David C Cook in 2013 © J. Warner Wallace, ISBN 978-1-4347-0469-6

The Team: Don Pape, John Blase, Renada Arens,
Caitlyn Carlson, Nick Lee, Karen Athen.
Cover Design: Amy Konyndyk
Cover Images: Shutterstock

Printed in the United States of America
First Edition 2014

5 6 7 8 9 10 11 12 13 14 15

031419

ALIVE

INVESTIGATING THE RESURRECTION

I was a committed atheist when I first heard a pastor preach a sermon that described the resurrection of Jesus. This pastor seemed to actually believe Jesus rose from the dead and was still alive today. I assumed it was just another example of "blind faith"; another well-intentioned church leader believing something for which he had no supporting evidence. Worse yet, I suspected he possessed an "unreasonable faith" and trusted something *in spite of* the evidence.

I was familiar with the rules of evidence and the process by which we can determine the truth about past events. As a detective, I was doing this for a living. I decided to investigate the resurrection as I would any unsolved case from the distant past. My journey led me out of atheism to the truth of Christianity. As I applied my skills as a detective, I became more convinced that the New Testament gospel accounts reliably describe the life, ministry, crucifixion, and resurrection of Jesus. I bet you'll come to the same conclusion if you take the time to examine the evidence and the explanations offered for the resurrection of Jesus.

THINKING LIKE A DETECTIVE

As a detective, I often employ a methodology known as *abductive reasoning* (also known as "inferring to the most reasonable explanation") in order to determine what I have at a crime scene. I collect all the evidential data and make a mental list of the raw facts. I develop a list of the possible explanations that might account for the scene in general. Finally, I compare the evidence to the potential explanations and determine which explanation is, in fact, the most reasonable inference in light of the evidence.

As it turns out, detectives aren't the only people who use abductive reasoning in an effort to figure out what really happened. Historians, scientists, and all the rest of us (regardless of vocation or avocation) have experience as detectives. In fact, most of us have become accomplished investigators as a matter of necessity and practice, and we've been employing abductive reasoning without giving it much thought.

I had a partner once who gave me a bit of parental advice. Dave was a few years older than I was, and he had been working patrol for many years. He was a seasoned and salty officer, streetwise, cynical, and infinitely practical. He had two children who were already married when mine were still in high school. He was full of sage advice (along with some other stuff).

"Jim, let me tell ya something about kids. I love my two boys. I remember when they were in high school and used to go out with their friends on the weekends. I would stay up late and wait for them to come home. As soon as they walked in the door I would get up off the couch and give them a big hug."

This struck me as a bit odd, given what I knew about Dave. He seldom exposed a sensitive side. "Wow, Dave, I have to tell you that I don't usually think of you as a touchy-feely kind of guy."

"I'm not, you moron," Dave said, returning to form. "I hug them as tightly as possible so I can get close enough to smell them. I'm not a fool. I can tell if they've been smoking dope or drinking within seconds."

You see, Dave was an evidentialist, and he applied his reasoning skills to his experience as a parent. The smell of alcohol or marijuana would serve as evidence that he would later take into consideration as he was evaluating the possible activities of his children. Dave was thinking abductively. I bet you've done something similar in your role as a parent, a spouse, a son, or a daughter.

DISTINGUISHING BETWEEN POSSIBLE AND REASONABLE

All of us have learned the intuitive difference between possible and reasonable. When it comes right down to it, just about anything is possible. You may not even be reading this book right now, even though you think that you are. It's possible that aliens covertly kidnapped you last night and have induced a dreamlike, out-of-body, extra-terrestrial hallucination. While you think this experience of reading is real, you may actually wake up tomorrow morning to discover yourself in an alien spaceship. But let's face it—that's not reasonable, is it?

While it's interesting to imagine the possibilities, it's important to return eventually to what's reasonable, especially when the truth is at stake. That's why judges across the land carefully instruct juries to refrain from what is known as *speculation* when considering the explanations for what has occurred in a case. Jurors are told that they "must use only the evidence that is presented"[1] during the trial. They are told to resist the temptation to consider the attorney's opinions about unsupported possibilities and to ignore unsupported speculation whenever they may hear it.

Judges also tell jurors to resist the impulse to stray from the evidence offered and ask questions like "What if …?" or "Isn't it possible that …?" when these questions are driven by evidentially unsupported speculation. They must instead limit themselves to what's reasonable in light of the evidence that has been presented to them.

In the end, our criminal courts place a high standard on reasonableness, and that's important as we think about the process of abductive reasoning. This rational approach to determining truth will help us come to the most reasonable conclusion in light of the evidence. It can be applied to more than criminal cases; we can apply the process of abduction to our spiritual investigations as well. But first, let's examine the concept with a real-life example from the world of homicide investigations.

ABDUCTIVE REASONING AND DEAD GUYS

Let's use the example of another death scene to fully illustrate the process. You and I have been called out to a "dead-body scene"—a location where a deceased person has been discovered and the circumstances seem rather suspicious. While scenes like this are sometimes homicides, they are often less sinister; there are a few other explanations. Deaths fall into one of four categories: natural deaths, accidental deaths, suicides, or homicides. It's our job to figure out which of the four explanations is the most reasonable in the following scenario.

We have been called to the scene of a DBR (a "Dead Body Report") to assist patrol officers who have already arrived and secured the location. Here are the facts we are given when we enter the room: A young man was discovered on the floor of his apartment when his roommate returned from work. The man was lying facedown. The man was cold to the touch, nonresponsive, and stiff. Okay, given these minimal facts, it is clear that we actually do have a dead guy, but which of the four potential explanations is most reasonable given the facts? Is this death a natural death, an accident, a suicide, or a homicide?

Dead Man
Lying Facedown

natural death
accidental death
suicide
homicide

Given the minimal facts so far, all four of the potential explanations are still in play, aren't they? Unless we have something more to add evidentially, it will be difficult to decide if this case should be worked as a homicide or simply documented as something other than criminal. Let's change the scenario slightly and add a new piece of evidence to see if it will help. Imagine that we entered the room and observed that the man was lying in a pool of his own blood and that this blood seemed to be coming from the area of his abdomen (under his body).

These are the new minimal facts: (1) A man is dead, (2) lying facedown on the floor, (3) in a pool of blood that seems to be coming from the

front of the man's lower abdomen. Given this new
set of facts, is there any direction our investigation
might take? Are any of our four explanations more
or less reasonable?

Given the new evidence, we may be comfort-
able in removing the natural-death explanation
from our consideration. After all, what kind of
natural event in the human body would cause
someone to bleed from his lower abdomen? Since
the man lacks an orifice in that location from
which to bleed naturally, this does seem to be an
unfounded conclusion to draw; a natural death
might be possible, but it isn't reasonable.

What about the other three explanations?
Could this still be an accidental death? Sure, the
man could have tripped and fallen on something
(we wouldn't know this until we turned him over).
What about a suicide or a homicide? It seems
that these three remaining explanations are still
reasonable in light of what limited evidence we
have about this case. Until we learn a bit more, it

will be difficult to decide which of these final three options is the most reasonable.

Let's add a new dimension to the case. Imagine that we enter the room and see the man lying on the floor in a pool of his own blood, but now we observe a large knife stuck in his lower back.

This presents us with a new set of facts: (1) The man is dead, (2) lying facedown on the floor, (3) in a pool of blood, and (4) there is a knife stuck in his lower back. The presence of a knife in the victim's back seems to eliminate as unreasonable the conclusion that he died accidentally. It's hard to imagine an accident that would account for this fact; an accidental death might be possible but it's not reasonable. If nothing else, the presence of the knife most certainly affirms the unreasonable nature of a natural death, doesn't it? The most reasonable remaining explanations are either suicide or homicide, and suicide seems less and less likely, given the fact that the victim's wound is located on his back. But since the wound is located in the lower portion of his back (within his reach), let's leave this option on the table for now.

Imagine, however, that a new fact has entered into our scenario. Imagine that we discover three extra wounds on the victim's upper back, in addition to the one we observed earlier.

Dead Man
Lying Facedown
Pool of Blood
Knife in Back
Multiple Stab Wounds

natural death
accidental death
suicide
homicide

Our fact list now includes: (1) A man who is dead, (2) lying facedown on the floor, (3) in a pool of blood, (4) with multiple knife wounds on his back. Our reasonable explanations are dwindling, aren't they?

In this situation, natural death, accidental death, and suicide seem out of the question. While someone may argue that they are still possible, few would recognize them as reasonable. The most reasonable conclusion in light of the evidence is simply that this man was murdered. As responsible detectives, you and I would have no choice but to initiate a homicide investigation.

AN ANCIENT DEATH-SCENE INVESTIGATION

Now it's time to apply this form of reasoning to a death scene that has been the topic of discussion for over two thousand years. What happened to Jesus of Nazareth? How can we explain His empty tomb? Did His disciples steal His body? Was He only injured on the cross and later recovered? Did He actually die and resurrect from the dead? We can approach these questions as detectives, using abductive reasoning.

The question of Jesus's fate might be compared to our dead-body investigation. We examined our death scene by first identifying the characteristics of the scene (the facts and pieces of evidence). We next acknowledged a number of potential explanations that might account for what we observed. Let's apply that same approach to the issue of the alleged death and resurrection of Jesus.

Dr. Gary Habermas and Professor Mike Licona have taken the time to identify the "minimal facts" (or evidences) related to the resurrection. While there are many claims in the New Testament related to this important event, not all are accepted by skeptics and wary investigators. Habermas and Licona surveyed the most respected and well-established historical scholars and identified a number of facts that are accepted by the vast majority of researchers in the field.

They limited their list to those facts that were strongly supported (using the criteria of textual critics) and to those facts that were granted by virtually all scholars (from skeptics to conservative Christians). Habermas and Licona eventually wrote about their findings in *The Case for the Resurrection of Jesus.*

As a skeptic myself, I formed a list of New Testament claims as I first investigated the resurrection. When I was an unbeliever, I found four of Habermas and Licona's minimal facts to be the most substantiated by both friends and foes of Christianity:

1. Jesus died on the cross and was buried.
2. Jesus's tomb was empty, and no one ever produced His body.
3. Jesus's disciples believed that they saw Jesus resurrected from the dead.
4. Jesus's disciples were transformed following their alleged resurrection observations.

You'll notice that none of these "minimal evidences" necessitate that Jesus truly rose from the dead. There may be any number of explanations that account for these facts (we'll get to those in a moment). This is simply a list of evidences that most scholars (believers and unbelievers alike) would accept and all of us (believers and unbelievers alike) must explain. As I examined these bare-bones claims related to the resurrection, I assembled the possible explanations that have been historically offered to account for them (employing the process of abductive reasoning). I quickly recognized that every one of these explanations had its own deficiencies and liabilities (including the classic Christian account). Let's take a look at the potential explanations and list their associated difficulties.

THE DISCIPLES WERE WRONG ABOUT JESUS'S DEATH

Some skeptics have offered the possibility that the disciples were mistaken about Jesus's death on the cross. They propose that Jesus survived the beating (and the crucifixion) and simply appeared to the disciples after He recovered.

THE PROBLEMS

While this proposal seeks to explain the empty tomb, the resurrection observations, and the transformation that occurred in the lives of the apostles, it fails to satisfactorily explain what the disciples observed and experienced when they pulled Jesus from the cross. It's been my experience that witnesses who first come upon the dead body of someone they care about quickly check for the most obvious sign of life. Is the person who was injured still breathing? This test is simple and effective; everyone is capable of performing it, and even those who know nothing about human biology instinctively resort to it. It's also been my experience that three conditions become apparent in the bodies of dead people: temperature loss, rigidity, and lividity. Dead people lose warmth until they eventually reach the temperature of their environment. They begin to feel "cold to the touch" (this is often reported by those who find them). In addition, chemical reactions begin to take place in the muscles after death occurs, resulting in stiffening and rigidity known as *rigor mortis*. Dead people become rigid, retaining the shape they were in when they died. Finally, when the heart stops beating, blood begins to pool in the body, responding to the force of gravity. As a result, purple discoloration becomes apparent in those areas of the body that are closest to the ground. In essence, dead bodies look, feel, and respond differently than living, breathing humans do. Dead people, unlike those who are slipping in and out of consciousness, never respond to their injuries. They don't flinch or moan when touched. Is it reasonable to believe that those who removed Jesus from the cross, took possession of His body, carried Him to the grave, and spent time treating and wrapping His body for burial would not have noticed any of these conditions common to dead bodies?

In addition to this, the Gospels record the fact that the guard stabbed Jesus and observed both blood and water pouring from His body. That's an important observation, given that the gospel writers were not coroners or medical doctors. While I am certainly not a doctor, I've been to my share of coroners' autopsies, and I've spoken at length with coroner investigators at crime scenes. When people are injured to the point of death (such as the result of an assault or traffic accident) they often enter into some form of "circulatory shock" prior to dying (due to the fact that their organs and body tissues are not receiving adequate blood flow). This can sometimes result in either "pericardial effusion" (increased fluid in the membrane surrounding the heart) or "pleural effusion" (increased fluid in the membrane surrounding the lungs). When

Jesus was pinned to the cross in an upright position following the terrible flogging He received, it's reasonable to expect that this kind of effusion might have taken place in response to the circulatory shock He suffered prior to dying. These fluids would certainly pour out of His body if He were pierced with a spear. While the gospel writers might expect to see blood, their observation of the water is somewhat surprising. It is certainly consistent with the fact that Jesus was already dead when stabbed by the guard.

In addition to these concerns from the perspective of a homicide detective, there are other problems with the proposal that Jesus didn't actually die on the cross:

1. Many first-century and early second-century unfriendly Roman sources (i.e., Thallus, Tacitus, Mara Bar-Serapion, and Phlegon) and Jewish sources (i.e., Josephus and the Babylonian Talmud) affirmed and

acknowledged that Jesus was crucified and died.

2. The Roman guards faced death if they allowed a prisoner to survive crucifixion. Would they really be careless enough to remove a living person from a cross?

3. Jesus would have to control His blood loss from the beatings, crucifixion, and stabbing in order to survive, yet He was pinned to the cross and unable to do anything that might achieve this.

4. Jesus displayed wounds following the resurrection but was never observed to behave as though He was wounded, in spite of the fact that He appeared only days after His beating, crucifixion, and stabbing.

5. Jesus disappeared from the historical record following His reported resurrection and ascension and was never sighted again (as one might expect if He recovered

from His wounds and lived much beyond the young age of thirty-three).

THE DISCIPLES LIED ABOUT THE RESURRECTION

Some non-Christians claim that the disciples stole the body from the grave and later fabricated the stories of Jesus's resurrection appearances.

THE PROBLEMS

While this explanation accounts for the empty tomb and the resurrection observations, it fails to account for the transformed lives of the apostles. In my years working robberies, I had the opportunity to investigate (and break) a number of conspiracy efforts, and I learned about the nature of successful conspiracies. I am hesitant to embrace any theory that requires the conspiratorial effort of a large number of people over a significant period of time when they personally gain little or nothing by their effort. This theory requires us to believe that the apostles were transformed and emboldened not by the miraculous appearance of the resurrected Jesus but by elaborate lies created without any benefit to those who were perpetuating the hoax.

In addition to this concern from the perspective of a detective, there are other concerns that have to be considered when evaluating the claim that the disciples lied about the resurrection:

1. The Jewish authorities took many precautions to make sure the tomb was guarded and sealed, knowing that the removal of the body would allow the disciples to claim that Jesus had risen (Matt. 27:62–66).

2. Local people would have known it was a lie (remember that Paul told the Corinthians in 1 Corinthians 15:3–8 that there were still five hundred people who could testify to having seen Jesus alive after His resurrection).

3. The disciples lacked the motive to create such a lie.

4. The disciples' transformation following the alleged resurrection is inconsistent with the claim that the appearances were only a lie. How could their own lies transform them into courageous evangelists?

THE DISCIPLES WERE DELUSIONAL

Some skeptics believe that the disciples, as a result of their intense grief and sorrow, only imagined seeing Jesus alive after His death on the cross. These critics claim that the appearances were simply hallucinations that resulted from wishful thinking.

THE PROBLEMS

This proposal fails to explain the empty tomb and only accounts for the resurrection experiences at first glance. As a detective, I frequently encounter witnesses who are related in some way to the victim in my case. These witnesses are often profoundly impacted by their grief following the murder. As a result, some allow their sorrow to impact what they remember about the victim. They may, for example, suppress all the negative characteristics of the victim's personality and amplify all the victim's virtues. Let's face it, we all have a tendency to think the best of people once they have died. But these imaginings are typically limited to the nature of the victim's character and not the elaborate and detailed events that involved the victim in the past. Those closest to the victim may be mistaken about his or her character, but I've never encountered loved ones who have collectively imagined an identical set of fictional events involving the victim. It's one thing to remember someone with fondness; it's another to imagine an elaborate and detailed history that didn't even occur.

Based on these experiences as a detective, there are other reasonable concerns when considering

the explanation that the disciples hallucinated or
imagined the resurrection:

1. While individuals have hallucinations,
   there are no examples of large groups of
   people having the exact same hallucination.
2. While a short, momentary group hallucination may seem reasonable, long, sustained,
   and detailed hallucinations are unsupported
   historically and intuitively unreasonable.
3. The risen Christ was reportedly seen on
   more than one occasion and by a number
   of different groups (and subsets of groups).
   These diverse sightings would have to be
   additional group hallucinations of one
   nature or another.
4. Not all the disciples were inclined favor-
   ably toward such a hallucination. The
   disciples included people like Thomas,
   who was skeptical and did not expect
   Jesus to come back to life.

5. If the resurrection were simply a hallucination, what became of Jesus's corpse? The absence of the body is unexplainable under this scenario.

THE DISCIPLES WERE FOOLED BY AN IMPOSTER

Some nonbelievers have argued that an imposter tricked the disciples and convinced them that Jesus was still alive; the disciples then unknowingly advanced the lie.

THE PROBLEMS

While this explanation accounts for the resurrection observations and transformed apostles, it requires an additional set of conspirators (other than the apostles who were later fooled) to accomplish the task of stealing the body. Many of my partners spent several years investigating fraud and forgery crimes prior to joining us on the homicide team. They've learned something about successful con artists. The less the victim understands about the specific topic and area in which they are being "conned," the more likely the con artist will be successful. Victims are often fooled and swindled out of their money because they have little or no expertise in the area in which the con artist is operating. The perpetrator is able to use sophisticated language and make claims that are outside of the victim's expertise. The crook sounds legitimate, primarily because the victim doesn't really know what truly is legitimate. When the targeted victim knows more about the subject than the person attempting the con, the odds are good that the perpetrator will fail at his attempt to fool the victim.

For this reason, the proposal that a sophisticated first-century con artist fooled the disciples seems unreasonable. There are many concerns with such a theory:

1. The impersonator would have to be familiar enough with Jesus's mannerisms

and statements to convince the disciples. The disciples knew the topic of the con better than anyone who might con them.

2. Many of the disciples were skeptical and displayed none of the necessary naïveté that would be required for the con artist to succeed. Thomas, for example, was openly skeptical from the beginning.

3. The impersonator would need to possess miraculous powers; the disciples reported that the resurrected Jesus performed many miracles and "convincing proofs" (Acts 1:2–3).

4. Who would seek to start a world religious movement if not one of the hopeful disciples? This theory requires someone to be motivated to impersonate Jesus other than the disciples themselves.

5. This explanation also fails to account for the empty tomb or missing body of Jesus.

THE DISCIPLES WERE INFLUENCED BY LIMITED SPIRITUAL SIGHTINGS

More recently, some skeptics have offered the theory that one or two of the disciples had a vision of the risen Christ and then convinced the others that these spiritual sightings were legitimate. They argue that additional sightings simply came as a response to the intense influence of the first visions.

THE PROBLEMS

This proposal may begin to explain the transformation of the apostles, but it fails to explain the empty tomb and offers an explanation of the resurrection observations that is inconsistent with the biblical record. It's not unusual to have a persuasive witness influence the beliefs of other eyewitnesses. I've investigated a number of murders in which one emphatic witness has persuaded others that something occurred, even though the other witnesses weren't even present to see the event for themselves. But these persuaded witnesses were easily distinguished from the one who persuaded them once I began to ask for their account of what happened. Only the persuader possessed the details in their most robust form. For this reason, his or her account was typically the most comprehensive, while the others tended to generalize since they didn't actually see the event for themselves. In addition, when pressed to repeat the story of the one persuasive witness, the other witnesses eventually pointed to that witness as their source. While it's possible for a persuasive witness to convince some of the other witnesses that his or her version of events is the true story, I've never encountered a persuader who could convince everyone. The more witnesses who are involved in a crime, the less likely that all of them will be influenced by any one eyewitness, regardless of that witness's charisma or position within the group.

This theory also suffers from all the liabilities of the earlier claim that the disciples imagined the resurrected Christ. Even if the persuader could convince everyone of his or her first observation, the subsequent group visions are still unreasonable for all the reasons we've already discussed. There are many concerns related to the claim that a select number of persuaders convinced the disciples of resurrection:

1. The theory fails to account for the numerous, divergent, and separate group sightings of Jesus that are recorded in the Gospels. These sightings are described in great detail. It's not reasonable to believe that all these disciples could provide such specific detail if they were simply repeating something they hadn't seen for themselves.

2. As many as five hundred people were said to be available to testify to their observations of the risen Christ (1 Cor. 15:3–8). Could all of these people have been influenced to imagine their own observations of Jesus? It's not reasonable to believe that

a persuader equally persuaded all these disciples even though they hadn't actually seen anything that was recorded.

3. This explanation also fails to account for the empty tomb or the missing corpse.

THE DISCIPLES' OBSERVATIONS WERE DISTORTED LATER

Some unbelievers claim the original observations of the disciples were amplified and distorted as the legend of Jesus grew over time. These skeptics believe that Jesus may have been a wise teacher but argue that the resurrection is a legendary and historically late exaggeration.

THE PROBLEMS

This explanation may account for the empty tomb (if we assume the body was removed), but it fails to explain the early claims of the apostles related to the resurrection. Cold-case detectives have to deal with the issue of legend

more than other types of detectives. So much
time has passed from the point of the original
crime that it seems possible that witnesses may
now amplify their original observations in one
way or another. Luckily, I have the record of
the first investigators to assist me as I try to
separate what the eyewitnesses truly saw (and
reported at the time of the crime) from what
they might recall today. If the original record
of the first investigators is thorough and well
documented, I will have a much easier time
discerning the truth about what each witness
saw. I've discovered that the first recollections of
the eyewitnesses are usually more detailed and
reliable than what they might offer thirty years
later. Like other cold-case detectives, I rely on
the original reports as I compare what witnesses
once said to what they are saying today.

The reliability of the eyewitness accounts
related to the resurrection, like the reliability of
the cold-case eyewitnesses, must be confirmed

by the early documentation of the first investigators. For this reason, the claim that the original story of Jesus was a late exaggeration is undermined by several concerns:

1. In the earliest accounts of the disciples' activity after the crucifixion, they are seen citing the resurrection of Jesus as their primary piece of evidence that Jesus was God. From the earliest days of the Christian movement, eyewitnesses were making this claim.

2. The students of the disciples also recorded that the resurrection was a key component of the disciples' eyewitness testimony.

3. The earliest-known Christian creed or oral record (as described by Paul in 1 Corinthians 15) includes the resurrection as a key component.

4. This explanation also fails to account for the fact that the tomb and body of Jesus have not been exposed to demonstrate that this late legend was false.

THE DISCIPLES WERE ACCURATELY REPORTING THE RESURRECTION OF JESUS

Christians, of course, claim that Jesus truly rose from the dead and that the Gospels are accurate eyewitness accounts of this event.

THE PROBLEMS

This explanation accounts for the empty tomb, the resurrection observations, and the transformation of the apostles. It would be naive, however, to accept this explanation without recognizing the fact that it also has a liability that has been examined and voiced by skeptics and nonbelievers. The claim that Jesus truly rose from the dead presents the following concern and objection:

1. This explanation requires a belief in the supernatural: a belief that Jesus had the supernatural power to rise from the dead in the first place.

ABDUCTIVE REASONING AND THE RESURRECTION

I limited the evidence to four modest claims about the resurrection and kept my explanatory options open to all the possibilities (both natural and supernatural). The last explanation (although it is a miraculous, supernatural explanation) suffers from the least number of liabilities and deficiencies. If we simply enter into the investigation without a preexisting bias against anything supernatural, the final explanation accounts for all of the evidence without any difficulty. The final explanation accounts for the evidence most simply and most exhaustively, and it is logically consistent (if we simply allow for the existence of the supernatural in the first place). The final explanation is also superior to the other accounts (given that it does not suffer from all the problems we see with the other explanations).

If we approach the issue of the resurrection in an unbiased manner (without the naturalistic presuppositions) and assess it as we evaluated the dead-body scene, we can judge the possible explanations and eliminate those that are unreasonable. The conclusion that Jesus was resurrected (as reported in the Gospels) can be sensibly inferred from the available evidence, if we are simply open to the inclusion of supernatural explanations.

MOVING FROM THE MOST REASONABLE INFERENCE TO A DECISION TO TRUST

It's one thing to "believe that" Jesus rose from the dead and is who He said He was, but it's another to "believe in" Him as Savior. Every one of us, at some point in our investigation of the claims of Christianity, has to move from "belief that" to "belief in." I can remember when this happened for me. As a rebellious, self-reliant detective, I initially denied my *need* for a Savior, even though I accepted what the Gospels told me *about* that Savior. In order to take a step from "belief that" to "belief in," I needed to move from an examination of *Jesus* to an examination of *me*. As I read the Gospels for a second and third time and explored all of the New Testament Scripture, I began to focus more on what it said about *me* than what it said about *Jesus*. I didn't like what I saw. Over and over again, I recognized the truth about my own character, behavior, and need for forgiveness;

I began to understand my need for repentance. The facts about Jesus confirmed that He was the Savior; the facts about me confirmed my need to trust in Him for forgiveness. I was now ready to move from "belief that" to "belief in."

Maybe that's where you are right now—on a journey from "belief that" to "belief in." I'd like to offer a little encouragement. If Jesus rose from the dead and ascended into heaven as the eyewitnesses reported, He is alive today; He is God. As an atheist, however, I enjoyed being my own god; I liked being the only judge and jury I would ever require. I was unwilling to submit my authority to anyone or anything bigger than myself. As you examine the evidence for Christianity, ask yourself the same question I eventually had to ask of myself: "Am I rejecting this because there *isn't* enough evidence, or am I rejecting this because I don't *want* there to be enough evidence?" Are you denying the resurrection on evidential grounds or simply because you are stubbornly biased against anything supernatural or pridefully unwilling to submit your authority? If you're fair with the answer, you'll take an important step on your journey from "belief that" to "belief in."

NOTES

1. Judicial Council of California, *Judicial Council of California Criminal Jury Instructions*, CalCrim Section 104, accessed May 16, 2012, www.courts.ca.gov/partners/documents/calcrim_juryins.pdf.

CASE CLOSED?

A Detective Looks at the Claims of Christianity
This unique apologetic will help you understand
and articulate the truth of Christ like never before.

David C Cook
transforming lives together